REVIEWS

"A powerful, raw, and incredibly relatable deep dive into identity, conditioning, ego, external validation, and the slow unraveling that leads someone to finally question the life they built on autopilot."

Davey Lloyd - Mental Health Advocate

Kiani has lived every side of this story, and she delivers it with truth and precision. She's walked through despair, rebuilt herself from the ground up, and risen in business, mindset and spirit.

The principles she lays out in this book are real, practical keys for anyone who's ready to shift their life. If you feel trapped in the script society handed you, this book gives you the clarity and direction to write your own.

Kiani is a force. Her wisdom is matched by deep empathy because she's lived the climb herself. I'll be recommending this book to anyone stuck in the grind and searching for freedom.

Mark Halaar "Tarzan" – Survivor

"Kiani Mills aka Superstar delivers a raw, courageous, and transformative message for anyone ready to reclaim their power. The Purple Pill isn't just a book, it's a movement toward truth, wholeness, and radical self-leadership…"

Andrew Morello
– Winner of the First Australian Apprentice

THE PURPLE PILL

HOW TO BALANCE SUCCESS AND SELF IN A DIVIDED WORLD

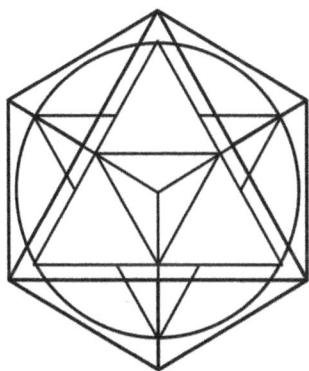

Kiani Mills

First published in Australia by Aurora House
www.aurorahouse.com.au

This edition published 2025
Copyright © Kiani Mills 2025

Typesetting and e-book design: Amit Dey (amitdey2528@gmail.com)
Cover design: Donika Mishineva (artofdonika.com)

The right of Kiani Mills to be identified as the Author of the Word
has been asserted in accordance with the Copyright, Designs and
Patents Act 1988.

ISBN NUMBER 978-1-923298-70-5 (paperback)

NATIONAL
LIBRARY
OF AUSTRALIA
A catalogue record for this
book is available from the
National Library of Australia

DEDICATION

This book is dedicated to Courtney Paige Mills
(26 October 1987 – 12 January 2025).
Loving sister.

ACKNOWLEDGEMENTS

Firstly, to me, ten years ago. The girl stuck in the Blue Pill.

I love her. I see her. I honour her. She fucking ROCKED. She survived better than most, and she is still such a huge part of me today. I wouldn't be here without her badass views and independent nature.

To my parents, Mum and Dad. I am who I am because of you. Thank you for the love, the lessons, and the guidance.

Mum, thank you for being a fierce, strong, hardworking woman who gave us kids everything we needed. Watching you do it all showed me that I can do it all, too. But I also want to pause here to honour what you sacrificed for us. You gave your life for us. Thank you.

To my beautiful kids. My biggest teachers in this lifetime. Who knows where my life would be if you hadn't come into my world! You are my WHY. You've kept me grounded, on track, laser-focused, and determined to give you the best life possible.

To my sister. My beautiful Courtney.

You left us on 12 January 2025, and your passing cracked me wide open. This book had been 'in progress' for five years, but it was in the deep, dark hole of grief, sitting on the couch, mourning you, that the words poured out of me. You guided them. Your spirit is in these pages. I miss you. I wish you were here. But I know you *are* here, woven into every word, every breath of this book.

To my brother, Kyle. You inspired the motivation to finish. You saw what I wanted to say and understood the words even before they were written.

To the publishing team at Aurora House. Thank you for seeing my vision and believing in this book.

And to my friends, family, mentors, spiritual healers, guides, and coaches … THANK YOU. Each and every one of you has been a part of this journey – holding me, shaping me, and reminding me of the power within me.

CONTENTS

PART 1

THE BLUE PILL -
RADICAL FREEDOM

CHAPTER 1

THE INDOCTRINATED IDENTITY

*The Hustle, The Grind,
and the Identity You Didn't Choose*

Let me ask you something upfront: Did you *choose* who you are – your personality? Or did you *inherit* it? Were you born with it, or were you raised into it? Because if you're anything like me, your personality wasn't simply downloaded like some self-aware, custom app. It was *handed to you* piece by piece, instilled in you year by year – and you absorbed it all, just like the good little sponge you were supposed to be.

It was shown to you, shaped over time by your parents, siblings, teachers, friends, weird uncles, awkward teenage relationships, and likely by a few episodes of *Home and Away* and *Neighbours*.

To explain it in another way: we are all, quite simply, the product of all the beautiful but unintentional fragments of beliefs, patterns, habits, and trauma that are passed down to us, bits and pieces of everyone we've ever met, everything we have ever absorbed, all that we have heard, and all that we have ever been told, ultimately creating the total of *us*, the perfectly imperfect mosaic of who we are.

This, my friends, is called 'indoctrination.'

Indoctrinate (verb):

To imbue with a usually partisan or sectarian opinion, point of view, or principle.

Especially: To teach or inculcate with a biased belief or ideology.

In short: To instil beliefs without encouraging independent thought or questioning.

Indoctrination begins at the ripe young age of birth and continues throughout our whole lives. Don't get me wrong – it isn't always bad. Most of the time it is wrapped in love, safety, and tradition.

Unfortunately, out of all the beautiful beliefs, patterns, habits, and traits that are passed down to us in childhood, we are inevitably too young to know the difference between those that are helpful and those that are a hindrance. After all, when we are little, we trust the big people in our lives. We want to be like them. Want to be accepted by them. Want to be loved by them.

And the big people, generally with no ill intent, are just trying to give us their version of love, safety, and tradition. Trying to show us the things they wish they had known, learned, or been shown. Or they're simply passing down the behaviours, patterns, beliefs, and traditions that *their* parents gave *them*.

So, you see, it's a cycle: our big people, learning from their big people, who learned from *their* big people, and so on. Passing down through the generations their version of truth. But actually, it isn't truth. It's programming.

We are all indoctrinated. Not because our parents were bad, or our teachers were cruel, but because systems thrive when people don't ask too many questions. When they follow the rules without wondering who wrote them or why.

Take family, for example. Parents, guardians, elders, and the beliefs, behaviours – even fears – they passed down to us, most of it unconsciously. We were told to be good, to work hard, to stay safe, to not cry, to not speak unless spoken to. These weren't choices. They were inheritances.

Then, there was school. A place where the rules were rigid and the books on the library shelf were pre-approved. We weren't invited to question the curriculum. We were told to memorise everything we were taught. Success meant silence. Good grades were given to the ones who complied, not the ones who coloured outside the lines. It was less about learning, more about conforming.

Sport was no different. Our coaches became our first bosses. They barked orders, rewarded discipline, and taught us to push through pain. Emotion was weakness. Injury was failure. We learned to override the body's whispers and obey the whistle. Winning was everything. Vulnerability? *Not welcome.*

Even the media was 'teaching' us. Every magazine cover, every movie, every princess waiting to be saved. The subliminal message? *Be beautiful. Be wanted. Be less.* And if you're too loud, too bold, too ambitious, you're a threat. *Tone it down, would you?*

Religion and culture layered yet more on top, with their rituals and rules, their scripts about right and wrong, about sin and salvation. We were told what to wear, who to be, and what to believe. Not by invitation, but by instruction. Deviation meant shame. Curiosity was dangerous.

And then we entered the workforce, where the indoctrination only got shinier. Success was measured in hours worked, emails sent, deals closed.

Your worth? Tied to your output.

Your value? Dependent on your title.

You were rewarded for burnout and celebrated for self-abandonment.

We absorb what we are praised for. We contort for approval. We learn how to keep the peace. We learn how to make people proud. And if we're really good at it? We become high-functioning adults who look successful on paper and feel *mildly dead inside.*

This is the water we are swimming in.

No one told us we had any other choice.

No one.

So, now that we have identified what indoctrination is, we can see or consider that maybe we aren't as messed up as we first thought. Maybe we aren't that crazy, and perhaps, just perhaps, there is still a chance for us yet! Maybe the parts of us that we don't quite understand are just simply the effects of our upbringing and conditioning that we are yet to shed light on. Maybe we *do* have a choice or an option to change, or decide to be something else, be someone else …

∽

Me? I didn't realise I was indoctrinated until it was far too late. When I say indoctrinated, of course, I don't mean in a cultish kind of way, but in the far more dangerous, socially acceptable kind of way. The kind where you think you're making your own decisions, until one day you look at your life and realise you've been living someone else's blueprint. By someone else's rules, someone else's expectations. And you don't even know who 'you' actually are beneath it all. You feel like a stranger in your own skin, unable to recognise who the hell you've become and how the hell you ended up here.

For me, the programming started early. Like it does for most of us.

I was the good girl. The helper. The overachiever. I tried my best to be 'perfect,' tried not to take up too much space, and I figured out pretty quickly that love and praise weren't unconditional. They were earned.

Be good. Get the gold star.

Don't cry. Don't question. Don't make a scene.

So, I became exceptional. At everything. At school. At sport. At shape-shifting – LOL. I labelled myself the 'chameleon,' knowing full well I was bending to everyone else's needs, wants, desires, and expectations, but ignoring my own.

It's funny, looking back. No one ever said, "You should sacrifice yourself for the betterment of others." But that's exactly what I learned and perceived to be true, from a very young age. I had no idea what I was doing. I suppose none of us do, really, and I guess this is why we learn these things later in life, so we can look back and think, "Ah-ha … I see it *now*!" Hindsight, the gift of retrospection!

This is what the Blue Pill teaches us. Highlights for us. Shows us. Brings to the surface.

You might remember the scene from *The Matrix*. Neo, faced with a choice: Take the Blue Pill and stay asleep in the illusion, plugged into the system and unaware, or take the Red Pill and wake up to the raw, unfiltered life beyond the veil.

Most people watch it and think, "Duh. Obviously, take the Red Pill."

But here's the kicker: most of us choose to take the Blue one. Repeatedly. Every single day.

We choose it whenever we say "yes" when we mean "no." We choose it whenever we chase success that doesn't satisfy us. We choose it whenever we hide parts of ourselves just to be accepted.

The Blue Pill isn't *one decision*. It's a way of life. An identity. It's the concrete jungle. The suits. The grind. The perfectionism.

It's waking up in the morning and checking your phone before your first breath, because you want to see those social media notifications that confirm you matter, or that people care. It's trading time for money. Self-worth for validation. Freedom for familiarity.

And I was fucking *amazing* at it.

I built empires on Blue Pill fuel. National companies. International speaking gigs. Designer heels. A diary so full there was no room left for myself, my family, or my sanity.

I had the media exposure. The staff. The glass offices. The *"Wow, Kiani, you're killing it!"* accolades.

And I was. I was killing it.

But I was also quietly killing parts of myself.

The parts that were soft. The parts that were still. The parts that were human.

Because in the Blue Pill world, emotion is weakness. Stillness is laziness. And softness? Softness is a liability. If you're not growing, you're dying. Literally … DYING!

So, I learned to be sharp. Strategic. Unshakeable.

I became the woman who never missed a beat, who held it all together. Who smiled on stage while falling apart in private.

There is a brilliant Taylor Swift song titled "I Can Do It with a Broken Heart." Now, no man would ever get close enough to me to break my heart, but gosh, did I break my own heart every single day.

'Cause I'm a real tough kid, I can handle my shit
They said, "Babe, you gotta fake it 'til you make it" and I did
Lights, camera, bitch, smile even when you wanna die
~~He said he'd love me all his life~~*
[*I said I'd love me all my life – Kiani Mills version]
But that life was too short
Breaking down, I hit the floor
All the pieces of me shattered as the crowd was chanting "More"
I was grinning like I'm winning, I was hitting my marks
'Cause I can do it with a broken heart (one, two, three, four).

Now, now. It wasn't all fake. I *did* love business. I *did* thrive on strategy. I *did* have dreams bigger than my postcode.

But I didn't know how to chase them without losing myself in the process. I didn't know how to chase them and be present as a mother. I *definitely* didn't know how to chase them while remaining grounded and able to maintain a healthy relationship, unless that relationship bent to my will at every single step, angle, and turn.

Why? Because I didn't *have* a self yet. I had a performance. I was playing a role - fantastically, maybe, but fake!

I was in control, and others had to fit in. I was in the driver's seat, and only if I allowed it would someone be permitted to join the party. I was a highly strung workaholic, stuck in survival mode, and living on 500 calories a day and office-fresh air-conditioned air.

My self-worth was measured by productivity. My success was measured in zeros. My nervous system was running on cortisol and caffeine.

And I was praised for it. Applauded. Celebrated.

So, I kept going. And going. *And going.*

Until the cracks became too obvious to ignore.

Until the mornings started to feel heavier. The relationships hollower. The smiles harder to fake.

Until I realised that I'd built everything *except* the life I actually wanted to live.

∽

The Blue Pill is seductive. It gives you structure, certainty, a clear path to success. Its only demands? *Just follow the rules. Just play the game. Just keep performing.*

But the cost? The cost is your truth.

It's the quiet ache that follows you from meeting to meeting. The guilt when you're with your kids, but your head is still in your emails. The voice in your gut whispering, "There must be more than this."

I heard that voice.

And at first, I ignored it.

I had a business to run. A reputation to protect. A bank balance to maintain.

But the voice didn't go away.

It got louder.

And eventually, I listened.

This is where my journey began. Not with a dramatic collapse or a grand awakening, but with a question:

What if everything I've built ... wasn't actually built for me?

That's when I began to see the Blue Pill for what it was.

A beautifully branded illusion. An ego-driven success story that wasn't really mine.

And it was time to unplug.

CHAPTER 2

SUCCESS, EGO, AND EXTERNAL VALIDATION

The Holy Trinity of Disconnection

Let's be honest.

There is a version of success that looks amazing and feels like shit. And most of us have bought into it … hook, line, and designer handbag.

It's the kind that fills your bank account while draining your joy. The kind that gets you standing ovations while you silently beg for someone to really *see* you. The kind where everyone else wants your life … and you secretly want OUT.

This chapter is about that kind of success.

The version we were sold. The version I mastered. The version that nearly broke me.

But before we go there, let's talk about what 'success' really means. Because if we don't redefine it, we'll keep chasing the version that's been fed to us but may not fulfil us at all.

Success (noun):

The achievement of a desired aim, goal, or outcome. Especially: To attain recognition, wealth, status, or influence as measured by external standards.

In short: The accomplishment of something deemed valuable; often defined by societal expectations but not always aligned with personal truth.

Success, as sold to us by the Blue Pill world, looks like this:

- Titles. Trophies. Status.
- 6 am alarms and 11 pm emails.
- A never-ending to-do list and a deeply underwhelming 'done' list.
- Performative ambition.
- More. Always more. More clients. More content. More followers. More figures. More proof that we matter.

More, more, more.

Until you're so full of everyone else's expectations that you're empty of your own presence.

It's subtle. It happens slowly over the years, as you watch others whom you aspire to be like. As you feed from those higher up the food chain. Watch the 'win' be so glorified that you decide you're willing to sell a kidney to make that *your* life, too.

And the worst part? You're completely unaware of who you're turning into.

Because you're getting praised. You're getting paid. You're getting likes and shares and offers and cries of "OMG, you're doing so well!"

But your soul is nowhere to be found.

The Blue Pill world is fast paced, (seemingly) relevant, trending, alluring, and *very* addictive. In order to succeed in it, we must unconsciously turn parts of ourselves off.

We must stay memorable, irreplaceable, and 'on top' at all times, or we risk missing out. 'FOMO' (fear of missing out) is a real thing. It results in action before alignment, impelling us to take risks before they are required. It asks us to abandon our core values and ethics for the sake of awards and accolades.

Let's define it clearly: **Success without alignment is just self-abandonment in heels.**

And I wore those heels well.

At my peak, I was managing multiple businesses. Speaking internationally. Hosting events. Mentoring women. Raising kids. Hosting a TV show. Interviewing international guests for my podcast. Smiling for the camera. Holding it all. Carrying it all. Achieving, always achieving.

But underneath that bright, high-functioning exterior was something darker: the constant fear that if I slowed down, if I stopped being impressive, I'd stop being worthy.

I didn't chase success because I was greedy. I chased it because I was scared. Scared to be still. Scared to be seen. Scared that if I took off the mask, no one would love what was underneath. Scared to be ME.

Not that I knew who 'me' was. I had never actually *been* just me. And what if I didn't like 'me'? What if she were weak, and slow, and emotional, and, worst of all, what if she cried?

NOPE, no way! Not ever going *there* ... no, thank you! Crying is not for me!

So, what did I do? I wrapped myself up, gave myself a big hug, put on my best suit, and let my best friend run the freaking show. Who is this 'best friend,' you ask? Well, she is strong, capable, driven, passionate, wins at all costs, powerful, and, some might say, remarkable.

So, let's meet her ... my old best friend and loyal body-guard: **The Ego.**

Now hear me out, please. The Ego gets a bad rap, but let's be fair. *She's not evil, she's clever.*

The ego is the part of you that figured out how to survive. How to be liked. How to win. She learns the rules and plays them better than anyone else.

She's also deeply afraid of being irrelevant.

For me, my ego was the high-achieving voice in my head saying, "You'd better prove yourself. Again. And again. And again."

She kept me sharp. Got me up at 4 am. Polished every word. Smiled through pain. Posted the win before I'd even processed the cost.

But here's the thing: she can't tell the difference between success and safety, so she'll have you working overtime for validation that doesn't actually land. She'll have you people-pleasing, over-functioning, over-committing – all in the name of control.

And when you try to slow down? She'll panic. Freak out.

Because if you're not being productive, what are you? If no one's clapping, do you even exist?

Remember, if you're not growing, you're dying. And when she thinks you're dying ... look out!

∾

It's funny the way people talk about ego these days. Everyone's 'transcending' it. Killing it. Rising above it. "The ego is bad." "The ego is the devil." Somewhere along the self-development highway, the ego became the villain of the story, something to shame, silence, or surgically remove.

But let me break it to you gently (and then not so gently): **You cannot kill your ego.**

You need it. We *all* do.

And honestly? Fantasy land isn't fun for anyone. Floating around pretending you're beyond your humanity? Not helpful. Not real. Not leadership. Go back to your oat milk matcha latte, with cold foam, caramel syrup, and a side of sunshine and unicorns!

Here's the truth: Your ego is not your enemy. Your ego is the part of you that *got you here.*

It's the voice in your head that says, "Look left and right before crossing the street."

It's the reason you put on clothes in the morning and proofread your emails before you send them. It's the reason you didn't scream that time in the boardroom, even though you wanted to.

It's the fire that pushed you onto the stage in the first place.

It's the protector. The mask. The armour.

The ego is your built-in survival system.

It learns fast. It adapts. It knows how to win in whatever environment you grew up in.

And for a long time? Mine was *really, really good* at winning.

She was strategic. Charismatic. Calculating, but kind enough to keep people close. She knew how to get what we needed to feel safe: approval, applause, achievement. She knew how to work a room. How to make the deal. How to take a hit and keep smiling.

My ego built companies. She got me through heartbreaks. She stood tall when my inner world was crumbling. She got the promotion, won the client, signed the contract, and smiled for the camera. She was unstoppable.

But here's the thing …

Just because your ego can drive the car doesn't mean she should be behind the wheel. Because when ego is driving, she's not following intuition. She's not checking in with the soul. She's not asking, "Is this what I *want*?" She's asking, "Will they *like* this?"

The ego's map is built entirely upon external terrain. What they'll think, how you'll look, who you need to be to be accepted.

So, while I was speeding down that road, burning fuel, breaking limits, overtaking milestones, I didn't realise I'd forgotten to check the destination.

And when I finally did, I realised I was nowhere near home.

That's the moment everything started to unravel. Not because I was weak or broken or ungrateful, but because I was finally strong enough to stop letting my ego run the show.

I didn't kill her. I thanked her. I gave her the passenger seat in the car. I just moved her out of the driver's seat.

That's when things started to shift. Not perfectly. Not instantly. But truthfully.

And that was the beginning of my return.

Ego is a part of us, so it's about bloody time we accept that and start to work with it, rather than against it!

There is only so long you can continue to push shit uphill!

If we were to wrap the Blue Pill into some sort of bundle, to me it would look like this:

1. EGO

The guy or gal running the show.

Ego (noun):

The part of the mind that mediates between the conscious self, the unconscious, and the external world.

Especially: A person's sense of self-esteem, self-importance, or identity.

In short: The mental construct of 'I' that seeks validation, protection, and control; often shaping how we see ourselves and how we want to be seen by others.

2. EXTERNAL VALIDATION

The Blue Pill's favourite currency.

External Validation (noun):

The act of receiving approval, recognition, or affirmation from outside sources, such as people, systems, or society.

Especially: Relying on others to define your worth, success, or identity.

In short: Seeking confirmation of value from the outside world, often at the expense of inner truth or self-trust.

Let me explain what this means in plain speak: External validation is when you check your phone to see who liked your post before you've even gotten out of bed in the morning. It's that hit of dopamine when someone says, "You're amazing." It's the invisible scoreboard you keep in your head.

And don't get me wrong – it feels good.

Until it doesn't.

Until your worth becomes tethered to that feedback. Until your self-esteem is on life support when the applause dies down. Until your decisions are shaped more by how they look than how they feel.

For years, I performed for the approval of strangers. I crafted my image. Sharpened my brand. I gave talks that made people cry, and then cried alone when no one was watching.

I let other people's perceptions decide how I felt about myself. And babe, that's not empowerment. That's enslavement with a side of high performance.

Eventually, it all caught up with me.

Not in one big crash, but in tiny, relentless ways. The late-night anxiety. The morning dread. The hollow victories. The kids saying, "You're always working." The mirror asking, "Is this really it?"

3. RADICAL FREEDOM

The Peter Pan syndrome.

Radical Freedom (noun):

The uncompromising state of inner liberation from external control, conditioning, or approval.

Especially: the ability to choose in alignment with your soul, rather than societal expectation or fear.

In short: Living a life designed by your truth – not by your trauma, your programming, or the need to please.

It sounds exhilarating, doesn't it?

That blue-sky flight of living life completely on your own terms, untethered, unapologetic, unfiltered. In the Blue Pill world, it was the highest aspiration.

I felt it in my independence and financial security. I was the highflyer, the relentless achiever, built for work and adrenaline. To me, life was meant to be lived at full volume: maximum effort, maximum reward. Success wasn't optional. It was mandatory.

This freedom came with steel nerves and leather seats – and a darker side. It tasted like late nights when ambition met with exhaustion. Alcohol became my best friend and escape, a fog that blurred the brilliance and the loneliness into one. My life became a series of high-stakes plays: I'd take the ultra-risk, chase the headline, push harder. Why? Because doing that made me feel alive. It felt like freedom.

To those in the Blue Pill world, freedom meant being unbound by fear. It meant power, wealth, fast cars, big offices. And yes, sometimes addictive behaviour came packaged in that same suit. But it gave me what I wanted: I was delivering results, fulfilling expectations, living the 'dream.'

Except, here's the thing. That kind of freedom isn't freedom at all.

Because in my pursuit of independence, I outsourced my humanity. In chasing autonomy, I anaesthetised my emotions. In building my empire, I built walls around my heart. I became good at the grind but disconnected from the grace.

This chapter doesn't end with a grand breakthrough. It ends with a decision: To stop living for applause. To stop being led by fear. To stop defining myself by numbers, nods, and next steps.

To finally ask: What if I didn't need to earn my worth? What if I could create a life that felt like *me*? The real me, not just a version of me that would be accepted.

And what if the next level of success wasn't about becoming more, but about *coming home*?

That's where I was headed next.

But first … I had to *feel*.

CHAPTER 3

THE HUSTLE THAT NUMBED ME

*The Currency of Capability and the
Cost of Disconnection*

You don't wake up one day and realise you're numb. It happens slowly.

You don't notice that you've stopped laughing from deep within your belly, or that your shoulders never fully drop anymore. You don't realise that the silence you used to enjoy has started to feel like a threat. You don't see it until it's too loud to ignore, until the moments that should be full of joy feel muted, like you're watching your life through soundproof glass.

That was me. I didn't feel empty; I felt efficient. I wasn't crying; I was focused. I wasn't breaking down; I was building an empire.

And for a while, it worked.

Being 'capable' became my identity. My currency. My superpower.

The hustle gave me something to hold onto. It gave me purpose, predictability, and most of all, *proof.* Proof that I was valuable. Proof that I was doing something with my life. Proof that I mattered.

But here's what no one tells you: hustle has a side effect.

It dulls your senses. It chips away at your softness. It numbs you from your own body.

Because when you're in survival mode, pleasure feels frivolous. Stillness feels unsafe. Simplicity feels suspicious.

I lived on caffeine and cortisol. I said "yes" when I meant "no." I worked weekends and called it "building my legacy." I was productive, magnetic, on-brand – always 'on.'

And underneath it all?

I was exhausted.

Not the kind of exhaustion a good night's sleep will fix. A deep, aching soul-tiredness that came from never switching off … and never simply being *with* myself.

I didn't know how to slow down. I didn't want to. Because if I slowed down, I might have to feel. And if I felt, I might fall apart. And if I fell apart, who would I even be without the 'doing' to distract me?

Again, "IF YOU'RE NOT GROWING, YOU'RE DYING!" And I couldn't risk dying.

I prided myself on being the woman who could handle anything. The one people called when the shit hit the fan. The one who kept it together, held the space, led the room.

And so, I became addicted to my own resilience.

Resilience, though, is a funny thing. It looks good on a motivational poster. But in practice? It can become a trap. A weapon we all too easily turn against ourselves.

Because if you're always 'fine,' always coping, always pushing through, who's tending to the version of you that's quietly crumbling?

My nervous system was screaming, and I told it to be quiet. My body begged for rest, and I answered it with another espresso. My intuition whispered, and I drowned her out with another to-do list.

The hustle numbed me. Not all at once, but gradually, like water smoothing down a jagged stone. Until I was so smooth, so polished, so high functioning that I'd forgotten what it felt like to really *feel*.

To feel joy. Grief. Lust. Stillness. Awe. To be moved by something that didn't have a deadline or an ROI.

And what was worse was that I wasn't alone.

I looked around and saw an entire generation of women wired the same way. Smart. Driven. Glowing on the outside, hollow on the inside. High-achieving zombies in designer blazers.

We were celebrated for our strength, but no one taught us softness. We were taught how to grow a business, but not how to *be* in the moment. We were praised for doing it all, but not for asking for help.

And so, we kept going. Until, that is, our bodies broke down. Until our relationships fractured. Until our children began to mirror back to us our disconnection.

I will never forget one pivotal occasion. It was a Tuesday morning, the sun already high as I climbed into the car with my daughter. She was bouncing with excitement, clutching a piece of paper in her hands – her latest drawing, covered in glitter and glowing with colour and six-year-old pride. She started talking before her seatbelt even clicked into place. Something about a rainbow. Something about a new friend. Something she was, clearly, desperate for me to hear.

I smiled. I nodded. I kept my eyes on the road.

But I wasn't listening.

I was already halfway through my mental to-do list. Staff issues. Settlement delays. A presentation I hadn't finished writing. An unanswered email from someone 'important.' My phone buzzed in the console beside me. Another message. Another obligation. Another string being pulled.

Then, I heard her voice again. Not playful this time. Quiet. Subdued.

"Mum … you're not listening."

I glanced over at her, startled. She wasn't angry. She wasn't upset. She was just stating a fact, like she was pointing out the weather.

You're not listening.

And in that moment, my heart broke. Because she was right.

I wasn't listening.

I wasn't there.

I hadn't been there for a long time, in fact. Not truly.

I had built an entire life in which I was always somewhere else, mentally, emotionally, and spiritually. I was either five steps ahead or ten steps behind, but rarely, if ever, in the *here and now*.

The truth hit me like a truck.

I didn't know how to *be* anymore without *doing*. I was a 'human doing,' not a human being.

'Doing' was how I survived. How I felt worthy. How I kept the machine running. I was the founder of a multimillion-dollar business, an employer of many, a trusted name in a fast-paced, high-stakes industry. I was the one who made it happen. Every time. No excuses.

I had become a master of the hustle. *And the hustle had become my home.*

People would praise me all the time: "Kiani, I don't know how you do it all."

And I'd smile, say thank you, throw in a self-deprecating laugh.

But inside, a voice whispered, *Neither do I.*

My body had been trying to tell me for years. Sleepless nights. Chronic back pain. Brain fog. A tightness in my chest I called 'just stress.' I ignored it all. I kept pushing. Because stopping felt terrifying.

Because if I stopped … what would I find?

There's a phrase I've come to love: *"High-functioning burnout."*

That was me.

I could still show up. Still deliver. Still sparkle on stage. Still reply to emails at midnight with flawless grammar. But I was running on fumes. And everyone around me – my clients, my team, my kids – was drinking from a well that was bone dry.

I had learned how to function brilliantly while quietly falling apart.

And no one saw it.

Because I didn't let them.

Because being the one who holds it all together had become my identity. My safety. My story.

The truth is, I was terrified that if I wasn't 'the capable one,' I would disappear completely. That if I didn't prove my worth every single day, I wouldn't be lovable. That if I slowed down, I'd lose it all.

So, I kept going. And going. *And going.*

Until I didn't know who I was anymore without a phone in my hand and a problem to solve.

The scariest part? I had been living like this for so long, I thought it was *normal.*

I thought this was just what it meant to be successful. A woman in business. A single mum with ambition and no safety net.

But what it *really* meant was that I had abandoned myself. Entirely.

I had stopped asking how *I* was. Stopped checking in. Stopped noticing the quiet ache in my chest every time I missed a school event, the guilt I swallowed when my kids saw the back of my laptop more than the whites of my eyes, the resentment I was carrying from being 'strong' for too long.

I had built a life that required me to betray my body, my boundaries, and my being on a daily basis.

And I was applauded for it.

Because we live in a world that celebrates burnout as bravery.

We are told that exhaustion is a badge of honour. That productivity equals worth. That if we just keep climbing the ladder, no matter the cost, we'll eventually find peace.

But what if peace isn't at the top? *What if it was never on the ladder at all?*

That Tuesday morning, in the car with my daughter, something shifted. Not dramatically. Not visibly. But internally, a tiny fracture formed in the dam.

Because when my daughter said, *"You're not listening,"* I didn't just hear her voice. I heard my soul. Quiet. Direct. Calling me home.

That was the beginning.

The beginning of a reckoning. Of asking myself the questions I had been too busy to consider …

Why am I really doing all this?

What am I running from?

What would happen if I stopped?

Everyone's always telling you to 'trust your gut.' I used to scoff at that, because mine was silent. It felt like nothing more than a void. I needed results, methods, proof – and I needed them *now*.

Feeling? That wasn't in my job description.

It was a sprint towards achievement, fuelled by adrenalised survival, starving my nervous system of serotonin and rest. Chronic stress kept me locked in fight-or-flight – and science confirms that when we live in this kind of petrified state, our mind–body connection shuts down.

That gut I was supposed to trust? It was on mute because my system was on high alert, assuming danger around every deadline and deal. The only things I *did* feel were the edges of an unending race: relentless drive, overwhelming pressure, fevered passion.

And though the successes multiplied – booked speaking gigs, podium finishes, profits – something was breaking inside me at exactly the same pace.

I told myself I couldn't stop. I couldn't slow down. *I'd made this bed; I would have to lie in it.*

But that self-sufficiency had come at a cost. I'd stopped asking for help – stopped even believing that anyone *could* help me – and shut everyone out.

Relationships   atrophied.   Vulnerability   vanished. Inside, I began to feel like the Ice Queen. Capable, polished, but cold. And it wasn't because I didn't *want* to connect; I was just too numb to know how. My defences felt safe, but the space inside me was hollow.

CHAPTER 4

THE ICE QUEEN

How Strength Became My Armour and
Softness Became My Threat

Not only did I begin to feel like the Ice Queen, but they actually *called* me the Ice Queen!

I used to wear that title as if it meant something powerful. As if it meant I was untouchable. Focused. Respected. I thought it meant I had mastered the art of composure. Until the day it cracked.

Let me tell you about the day the Ice Queen melted.

It was supposed to be a regular meeting – a professional catch-up between two business owners, nothing more. We'd met through a networking group, and he was coming into the office to film a quick promotional video and learn more about my business.

As he walked in that morning, I greeted him warmly – a hug hello, emanating bright energy, my usual self. We filmed. We laughed. We had lunch.

And then, with his fork halfway to his mouth, he looked up at me and said something that stopped time.

"I honestly thought you were a stuck-up bitch. I didn't even want to come today."

My smile dropped.

I blinked.

He kept talking, unaware of the impact his words were having.

"At those meetings, you just walk in like you own the room. You're on your phone, you don't talk to anyone. You just bark your directives and then disappear. There's no connection. No warmth. Just … ego."

My stomach turned.

I was stunned. Not because I was offended, but because I didn't recognise the person he was describing. That wasn't *me*, was it?

But as he spoke, I saw it. I saw *her*.

The Ice Queen.

She walked into every room with precision and intent. She was the one who arrived at 6:30 am, surreptitiously checking messages from her two kids at home, who were getting themselves dressed, making their own breakfasts, and walking to school alone. She was the one carrying the guilt of not being at home with them, while trying to hold together a business, a team, a life. She didn't have time for small talk. She was fighting to survive.

She walked into that room carrying giant rocks on her back, representing the social anxiety she was hiding, the fear of public speaking that she pushed down with a clenched fist. She felt like an imposter as she stood there at the front of a room filled with professional business owners, somewhere between ten and twenty years their junior. What the hell gave *her* the right to tell them how to run their businesses? She was in fear. She was in freeze. She wanted to *get the hell out of this uncomfortable space* the minute the event was over. So. She. Could. *Breathe.*

But no one saw that version of me. They saw the mask. They saw a fake. They felt an energy that was cold, rushed, distracted. And it left a stinging frostbite residue.

Over lunch, I explained all of this to him. The kids. The chaos. The emotional load. My social anxiety and fear of public speaking. I told him how hard those mornings were, how I never meant to come across as rude or self-important, how I was simply overwhelmed.

He sat in silence, stunned.

"I had no idea you were going through all of that."

Exactly. *No one ever does.*

And that's the thing about energy: It doesn't lie.

We think we can mask our anxiety with professionalism. We think we can bury our insecurity beneath 'busyness.' We think we can hide our hurt behind a façade of being 'on top of it all.'

But we can't.

Whether we realise it or not, we are always leaving an imprint.

That moment changed me. Not because I was embarrassed, but because it made me wonder: *How many people have walked away from an interaction with me feeling like that? How many people have experienced my stress as snobbery? How many people have mistaken my social anxiety for arrogance? How many hearts have I unintentionally frozen out?*

It was a sobering realisation.

That, even though my heart was soft, warm, full of love, my presence didn't always reflect that.

❦

My Ice Queen was riddled with ego. Even though she was hurting on the inside, the ego was protecting her and giving her the strength to stand up and keep going – even when she didn't want to or was afraid to. It was a perfect example of how our ego can help us, to a point.

I couldn't have stood up in those rooms – or overcome my social anxiety and fear of public speaking – if my ego hadn't been cheering me along. She held me, and she *pushed* me. She forced me to rise above those fears and anxieties. Why? Because she knew I was made for more.

Regardless of being numb and detached, I have always had an intrinsic belief that I was meant for more. Sounds egotistical, right? Well, I suppose it is. But it's deeper than me wanting to be a billionaire so I can flaunt my dollars, or drive fancy cars and show everyone on the gram. It isn't actually about me – even though I feel as though I have been shafted with the responsibility of undertaking 'it.' It's about service. It's about leaving a legacy. It's about changing the world, no matter how small the impact.

It's also wrapped in a belief that *I can't be the only one feeling this way and wishing to do more*. Even though fear is lonely, it doesn't mean we are alone in it. There are billions of people on earth, and the chance that I am so special that I am flying through this thing solo is, in fact, impossible. I knew 'my people' were out there … I knew that I could find them. I knew that I could find *myself* and become the version of me who could walk into a room and light it up with positive energy.

I knew my heart was good.

I just had to find my way through the mess.

And so began the work.

The undoing.

The melting.

I became obsessed with understanding the energy I bring into a room. I started studying communication, body language, trauma responses, somatics. I learned how to regulate my nervous system before walking into a meeting. I began listening more, softening more, being *with* people more, not just doing things *for* them.

And as I thawed, something beautiful happened. *The world around me softened, too.*

People began to lean in. Connections deepened. Clients became friends. Strangers became allies. I wasn't just respected anymore. I was *felt*. Seen. Loved.

And, perhaps more importantly, I felt others more deeply, too.

The Ice Queen was never the villain, I realised. She was just tired. Scared. She didn't know how to ask for help. She didn't know how to be both powerful *and* vulnerable. So, she built a fortress instead.

But fortresses keep *everyone* out. Even the people who want to love you.

And so now, when I walk into a room, I remind myself …

Let them feel your warmth.

Let them see your humanity.

You don't need to prove your worth anymore. You already are.

The Ice Queen didn't die. She simply learned how to feel again.

PART 2

THE RED PILL -
RADICAL EMPATHY

CHAPTER 5

THE FALL FROM GRACE

When the Cracks Became Canyons and
I Finally Let It All Crumble

E very perfectly curated life has a fault line.
And mine? Mine had been there all along, hidden beneath the glossy exterior, behind the Instagrammable moments, nestled between the meetings and the milestones and the motivational quotes.

I didn't see it.

Or maybe I just didn't want to.

Because admitting that something was off felt dangerous. It felt like betrayal. A betrayal of the image, the identity, and the version of me that everyone admired.

But cracks don't care about your image. They don't care about your plans, your titles, your client list, or your revenue streams.

Cracks widen.

And one day, they split.

My fall from grace wasn't like a dramatic movie scene. There was no big argument and subsequent tear-fuelled, wine-drinking, cheese-eating binge to a melancholic piano soundtrack. No mid-aisle meltdown in Woolies. (Although, that *very* nearly happened once in the frozen section – and to be fair, probably a few more times, too!)

It was quieter than that.

In fact, it looked like nothing, really. A silence. A void. A feeling of being lost even when surrounded by people. A sense that the lights were on, but no one was home.

It was waking up and not recognising my own reflection … not because my face had changed, but because I couldn't connect to the woman staring back at me.

Who was she, really, without the goals to chase? Without the applause to fill the silence? Without the inbox full of other people's needs?

I had spent so long being everything for everyone that I had no idea how to simply be … me.

I thought I was doing all the right things. The vision board. The hustle. The systems. The personal development books stacked on my bedside table like trophies of my effort.

But something was off.

Deeply off.

And it wasn't just that I was tired. I wasn't just 'in a funk.' I was unravelling. Silently. Subtly. Completely.

And the weirdest part? I was still functioning. Still doing it all. Still smiling, delivering, achieving.

But the gap between what I was doing and what I was feeling had become unbearable.

It felt like I was floating above my life, watching it happen. Watching *me* happen, and thinking, "Is this it? Seriously?"

That's the thing about spiritual awakenings. No one tells you how inconvenient they are.

They don't schedule themselves in between school pick-up and Monday's sales meeting. They don't arrive politely. They crack you open in the middle of your perfectly timed routine. They show up when you've done everything right and still feel completely *wrong*.

It started as a whisper. A question I couldn't un-hear.

What if I don't want this anymore?

What if I never did?

What if the life I've built isn't even *mine*?

I remember sitting in my car one afternoon after a big strategy meeting. On paper, it had been a win. We'd hit the goals. The team was pumped; the future looked bright.

Yet I just ... sat there. Staring into space. Numb.

Thinking, "How did I end up here?"

It's not that I wasn't proud of my achievements. I *was*. But something was missing, and I didn't know what. I just knew that whatever it was, it wasn't going to be in the next meeting, or the next goal, or the next trip to Officeworks to buy highlighters I didn't need.

I drove home that day, walked into my house, took off my shoes, sat on the floor ... and wept. Not loudly, not dramatically, but quietly, shockingly. The kind of crying where the tears just fall of their own volition. Without your permission. No theatrical sobbing or wailing. Just a kind of deep, surrendered knowledge.

The knowledge that something had to change.

The knowledge that I couldn't keep living a life that looked good but didn't *feel* good.

The knowledge that I had to fall – and I had to let myself.

And like any true fall from grace, it wasn't linear, it wasn't clean, it wasn't cute. There were days when I felt liberated and days when I questioned everything. There were moments of deep peace followed by periods of panic. There were journal entries, voice notes to myself, long drives in silence, and more existential Googling than I care to admit.

But something inside me was waking up.

And no matter how scary it felt, I knew, deeply knew, that I could never go back to sleep.

This was the beginning of the Red Pill. Of surrender. Of shedding. Of facing the grief for the woman I had built and making space to meet the woman I had buried beneath her.

She was coming.

And she was about to change *everything*.

Empathy (noun):

The action or capacity of understanding, being aware of, being sensitive to, and vicariously experiencing the feelings, thoughts, and experiences of another person.

Let's break it down into plain English: it's walking in someone else's shoes. Not just imagining their story but feeling their knock on your own heart. Making space for their pain, their joy, their contradictions, without turning away. Empathy isn't just caring; it's the ability to feel that care, deeply and fully, with that person.

CHAPTER 6

THE WORK BEGINS

From Cracking to Cracking Open ...
The Start of Rebuilding Me

So ... what do you do when you've built an empire on the wrong foundation?

Do you burn it down? Maybe. Or maybe not. It depends on the individual, I suppose.

Me? I got curious.

I started asking the questions I'd been too busy, too scared, too 'together' to ask:

Who am I underneath all of this? What do I want that I haven't admitted? Where am I performing instead of living?

And the biggest one of all ...

What the fuck do I actually FEEL?

(Which at first, admittedly, was mostly, "Tired. And maybe hungry?" Baby steps!)

The work began not with answers, but with permission.

Permission to not have it all together. Permission to cry and not hide the evidence. Permission to be seen in the act of unravelling, not just in the triumph of achievement.

And having granted myself that permission, I began to meet myself. Not the polished, public-facing, Power-Point-clicking version of me. But the real one. The one who didn't always know what to say. The one who sometimes overshared. The one who was exhausted but hopeful.

I signed up for workshops I had once rolled my eyes at. I meditated … and hated it … and then meditated again. I journalled until my wrist hurt. I went to breathwork classes and cried on yoga mats in rooms full of strangers with names like 'River' and 'Starlight.'

And I started learning that healing doesn't necessarily look like floating through the forest in a linen robe. It can look like sobbing in your car outside Woolies, yet still remembering to buy the damn almond milk.

I began noticing things I'd never been aware of before: the way my breath got shallow when someone questioned me. The way my chest tightened when I said "yes," but meant "no." The way I smiled even when I was deeply uncomfortable, just to keep the peace.

That's where the real work started. Not in the external world. But in my body. In my nervous system. In my truth.

I learned to sit with discomfort without running from it. I practised saying "no," even when my voice trembled. I let people see me messy, unfiltered, mid-process.

And it wasn't graceful. There were awkward moments and ugly crying sessions – and an alarming number of voice notes sent to my best friend that started with, "Okay, hear me out …"

But beneath the mess, I was meeting something real.

Me.

And she wasn't broken. She was just buried. Buried under years of expectation, years of being in performance mode. Years of being the strong one, the capable one, the woman who never wavered.

And as I began to dig her out, I also started to rebuild.

Slowly, intentionally, with the kind of care I used to reserve only for others.

I learned that growth wasn't about becoming someone new; it was about remembering who I was before the world told me who to be.

The work didn't end when I found the answers. The work *began* when I finally got brave enough to ask the questions.

And let me tell you something. If you're reading this thinking, "Shit … I might be in that place, too,"… then, good.

That means something in you is waking up.

And trust me, love … that's where the magic happens.

❦

When I spoke of indoctrination in the Blue Pill world, I was talking about silent control – the subtle conditioning that had shaped me, the rules I'd never questioned, the roles I'd fallen into without awareness, the performance I'd worn like armour. That world was built on following, scripting, and looking outside for approval.

The **Red Pill** is everything the Blue Pill is not. If Blue teaches obedience, Red teaches **agency**. If Blue feeds on hierarchy and conformity, Red feeds on **critical thinking**, curiosity, and questioning. It awakens you to your own power, your capacity to choose beyond the scripts.

The Blue Pill means having your identity handed to you on a silver platter. The Red Pill means building your own identity, one belief, one feeling, one truth at a time.

Blue asks, "Are you doing enough?" Red asks, "Are *you* enough?"

The Blue Pill world had taught me to swallow stories handed to me before I'd even learnt how to question them. Of course, like any coin, the Blue Pill had two sides: it had given me structure, ambition, security, and, while it had cost me connection, it had also paid the bills, put food on the table, and taught me how to win. It had propelled me into big offices, designer wardrobes, and a lifestyle many simply dream of. It had rooted me in competence and showed me I *could*.

Whereas Blue had given me confidence, Red forced me into an emotional wilderness. Its gifts? Radical empathy, purpose, intuition, spiritual clarity, and a deep rooting in my feminine essence. Its challenges? They were real. Disorientation, isolation, questioning, fierce emotional purging.

As people who've walked the spiritual path warn, this awakening often brings a kind of mental 'redness' – confusion, existential despair, even spiritual bypassing – using spirituality to avoid the real emotional work, like when we build castles in the sky to hide from our houses that are burning.

The Red Pill is the opposite of conformity. Whereas Blue asks, "Are you doing enough?" Red queries, "Are you *feeling* enough?" It shifts the question from external metrics to internal truth. Blue is a script; Red is improvisation. It is the antidote to indoctrination, an awakening of hunger for *your* voice rather than a borrowed one.

The Red Pill isn't just wondering; it's *demanding* honest presence, even if there's no applause at the end. It's moving from productivity to presence, susceptibility to sovereignty. But, in shifting away from performance, it asks for something deeper: it asks you to *feel*. And that isn't always rosy.

In the Blue Pill world, what you see is what you get: 9-to-5 routines, steel-and-concrete jungles, boardroom battles, and back-to-back efficiency. The positives are obvious: **drive, determination, passion, recognition**. You're a high-flyer who gets things done. You're the person others can rely on to deliver. On the flipside, it invites ego-driven performance, endless comparison, emotional disconnection. It numbs your senses, dulls your intuition, and reduces life to a scoreboard: *money, promotions, status*. There's comfort, but there's compromise.

Its mirror image, the Red Pill, brings **compassion**, **empathy**, **love** … a deep, raw connection to self, others, and the world. You enter a realm where *being* feels more alive than *doing*. You learn to *feel* again, to connect authentically, to work from compassion rather than ambition. Yet Red-Pill living isn't always rosy. As the heart expands, so too does your sensitivity. You can become **disorganised**, untethered by schedules and control. Financial literacy may slip, replaced by a blind trust that life will sort itself out. And, in your newfound empathy, you may find yourself **taking on others' pain**, absorbing what doesn't belong to you.

In a nutshell:

- The **Blue Pill** supported me. It brought comfort, identity, and stability. But it also numbed me.
- The **Red Pill** shook me awake. It invited me into feeling, presence, empathy. But it sometimes left me dizzy, untethered, struggling to find a new rhythm.

Both were necessary. Both had their checks and balances.

Both worlds serve us, and both limit us. The question isn't: "Which is better?" **It's: "Which part of you needs to be *seen* and *integrated* now?"**

I needed Blue to survive, but I needed Red to *live*. And as I stood between them, wavering, not knowing which way to step, I had a flash of insight.

Why did it have to be one or the other? Why not find a better balance?

Why not take the best from both and integrate them into … *the Purple Pill?*

In that instant of realisation, everything shifted. Questions overwhelmed answers. Layers of conditioning began to peel away. Where once there was compliance, there began to be inquiry. Where once I accepted the gospel of hustle, I started asking myself: *Why did I chase that? Who said I had to? What if there was another way?*

For me, the Red Pill wasn't about rejecting society as a whole. It was about recovering *my* society, from inside of me, layer by layer. It was about moving from indoctrination – which thrives on submission and unexamined roles – to **enlightenment**, **freedom**, and **radical awakening**.

When I stepped through that door, I didn't find emptiness. I found myself. Not a polished woman branded by achievement, but a messy, feeling, flawed human being who *belonged* to herself again.

But first, of course, I had to navigate my way through the raw, disorienting realness of the Red Pill.

That's the moment the real journey began.

CHAPTER 7

NAVIGATING THE RED PILL

*Awakening, Awareness, and the
Reckoning of Truth*

If the Blue Pill is the illusion, then the Red Pill is the reality you didn't want but can't unsee.

Taking the Red Pill doesn't look like some spiritual montage with crystals, candles, and a soundtrack by Florence and the Machine. It looks like being slammed with the full, unfiltered truth of your life and realising: *Oh shit, I built this.*

It's like finally switching on the lights in a room you've been living in for years and seeing the dust, the clutter, the mould growing in the corners. You weren't *bad* for not seeing it. You just didn't know the light switch was there.

But now you do.

And once you see – really *see* – you can't go back.

That's the Red. It's raw. It's relentless. And it's the most liberating thing you'll ever do.

Because now? Now, we're not pretending anymore. Now, we're not clinging to old identities or forcing old narratives to fit. Now, we're facing it. All of it.

The guilt. The grief. The patterns. The projections. The parts of you that you swore were "just who I am" – which are really just trauma responses in expensive shoes.

My Red Pill moment didn't happen in a temple or on a spiritual mountaintop. It happened in the most mundane, yet sacred, place of all: my own inner world.

It was the moment I stopped outsourcing my worth. The moment I questioned *everything* I'd been taught. The moment I said, "No more."

No more performing.

No more pleasing.

No more pretending to be fine when my soul was screaming.

And, let me be clear: it wasn't an elegant process. There were days when I felt like I was unravelling faster than I could catch the threads. Days when I grieved identities I didn't even like. Days when I questioned whether I was losing my mind … or, finally, *finding it.*

I realised I had learned that, in order to be *lovable,* I had to be *useful.* The way to be worthy was by being productive. The way to be safe was by being agreeable.

And even though I was unlearning all of it, I still had to face what had been built *on top of it.*

It was humbling. It was confronting. It was beautiful.

And it birthed something new:

Radical responsibility.

Responsibility (noun):

The state or fact of being responsible, answerable, or held accountable for something within one's duties, power, or control, whether a task, a trust, or a role.

In plain meaning: It's the calling you accept, whether raising kids, leading teams, or stewarding your own growth.

Or, to put it in your own voice: *Responsibility isn't punishment, it's ownership.* It's the choice to stand in the arena of your life and say, *"I'm here. I show up. I'm committed to this."* It is accountability tied with integrity, answering not just to others, but to your own North Star.

Not the hustle kind. Not the toxic positivity kind. Not the "just think happy thoughts and manifest a jet" kind.

The gritty, grounded, *grown-ass woman* kind. The kind where you say, "I did the best I could … and now I know better, I'll do better."

That's what the Red Pill asks of you. Not perfection. Not penance. Just truth.

It's not about burning everything down. It's about reclaiming what's real.

And when you do? You don't become someone else. *You come home to yourself.*

This chapter isn't about answers. It's about awareness.

The brave, beautiful moment, where you finally look in the mirror and say,

"Oh. There you are."

∾

Let's get real.

There's a version of spirituality that looks peaceful but feels like war.

And many of us have flirted with it. White robes, incense, retreats, silent suffering wrapped in serenity.

It's the kind that has you renouncing the world to find yourself. The kind that swaps ambition for isolation. That trades approval for awakening. The kind where everyone thinks you've transcended, whereas you're just dissociating in prettier packaging.

This chapter is about that kind of spirituality.

The version I stumbled into after the mask fell off. The version I dove into when the noise became unbearable. The version that stripped me down, one illusion at a time.

But, before we go there, let's talk about what 'awakening' actually means. Because if we don't ground it in reality, we'll keep floating off into fantasy.

Awakening (verb):

To rouse from sleep. To become conscious.

Especially: To become aware of something previously hidden or unconscious.

In short: To begin seeing the truth, often accompanied by discomfort, detachment, and the death of the familiar.

An awakening, as offered by the Red Pill world, looks like this:

Silence. Stillness. Slowness.

Nervous-system repair.

A deep grief for the life you used to love.

Awakening-induced identity death.

Surrender. Not performance.

Less 'rise and grind,' more 'sit and feel.'

Fewer followers, more presence.

Fewer checklists, more check-ins.

No longer building the life everyone else wants. Now dismantling the life that was never yours.

But here's the thing. It's not glamorous. It's not easy. It's not marketable.

It's one long, holy disintegration.

There's no spotlight. No praise. No stage. Just you, a mirror, and the inconvenient truth of who you've been pretending to be.

Let's name it clearly: *Awakening without integration is just another illusion wearing mala beads.* And I wore those beads well.

After building empires and identities, I left it all behind. Or at least I tried to.

I turned towards the Red.

I slowed down. Sat in ceremony. Cried with strangers. Hugged trees. Prayed at altars made of rose quartz and regret.

And it gave me something I never expected.

Not answers. Not enlightenment.

It gave me … *me*.

But first? It gave me heartbreak.

Because when you take the Red Pill, when you awaken, you can't go back to sleep.

You can't unknow the truth about the systems you served, the stories you swallowed, the self you shaped just to belong.

You start seeing indoctrination in high definition.

The manipulation in media. The abandonment in ambition. The disconnection in your dinner conversations.

You start questioning everything.

Why do we live like this?

Why do we work ourselves into the ground?

Why do we parent from fear and love from lack?

Why do we chase validation from systems that never cared about our wholeness?

And just when you think you've asked all the questions … You're hit with the biggest one:

Who the fuck am I without all of it?

That's when the second sacred force arrived. Not loud. Not proud.

Quiet. Earthy. World-altering.

RADICAL EMPATHY

Not the soft, surface-level kind. Not the "sending love" Instagram version.

I'm talking about the gritty, soul-wrenching kind of empathy that makes you *feel* everything.

Empathy (noun):

The ability to understand and share the feelings of another.

Especially: To be so attuned to another's experience that it touches your own being.

In short: The sacred act of connection that dismantles separation and invites unity.

Let me explain it in real talk: *Radical empathy is when you stop seeing 'them' and start seeing 'us.'*

It's when you look into the eyes of the person you once judged and see yourself.

It's when your pain becomes the portal to their pain.

It's when you realise we are not broken; we are just bruised from pretending we're whole.

For me, it started when I realised that every human I used to compete with, I now ached for.

The hustler? She's exhausted.

The influencer? She's insecure.

The CEO? He's terrified of stillness.

The angry mother? She's drowning.

The disengaged husband? He's disconnected from himself.

The rebel? She's hurting.

The victim? Just never felt safe.

I began to feel it all.

And not because I'd become enlightened, but because I'd finally stopped numbing myself.

Radical empathy didn't make me soft. It made me *real*. It cracked me open. It shattered my judgments. It showed me that healing is never just personal. It's collective.

And then came the final pillar. The one that held it all:

INTERNAL TRUTH.

The Red Pill's favourite currency.

Internal Truth (noun):

The deep knowing that arises from within, unshaped by outside opinions or expectations.

Especially: The authentic voice of the self, unfiltered by fear, people-pleasing, or programming.

In short: The voice beneath the noise.

Let me bring this home.

Internal truth is the quiet "no" you whisper when everyone else says, "yes."

It's the full-body "yes" to something that makes no logical sense but feels like freedom.

It's the choice to slow down when the world is screaming for speed.

It's the decision to walk away from what no longer fits, even if you built your whole life around it.

It's the knowledge that success doesn't have to come at the cost of your sanity.

That love doesn't have to feel like performance.

That peace doesn't have to be earned – it can be remembered.

For me, that truth came in moments. Sporadically. Never all at once.

It came in the space between my daughter's laughter and my to-do list.

In the breath I took before reacting.

In the way my body softened when I told my truth instead of telling people what they wanted to hear.

It came in the decision to stop 'performing' spirituality … and start *living soulfully*. No filter. No façade. No false humility.

Just the truth. My truth.

And it wasn't always pretty. It wasn't always marketable. *But it was mine.*

This chapter doesn't end with enlightenment. It ends with a return.

To body. To breath. To being.

To remembering that you were never broken. Just buried.

And now … *You rise.*

CHAPTER 8

RADICAL RESPONSIBILITY

Owning Your Shit Without Letting It Own You

In order to move forward, we must first go back … and this is the part where most people tap out.

Because this is where it gets *real.*

You've woken up. You've looked around. You've seen the systems, the conditioning, the masks you've been wearing, the lies you've been living, the stories you've been telling yourself on repeat like a bad Spotify playlist.

Now comes the question: *What the hell are you going to do about it?*

This is where the concept of **RADICAL RESPON-SIBILITY** enters the arena. And, let me tell you, it is not for the faint of heart.

This isn't the fluffy kind of self-help that says, "Every-thing happens *for* you, not *to* you" while ignoring systemic injustice, unprocessed trauma, and your very real lived experience. This is the messy, powerful, make-you-want-to-scream-and-then-exhale kind.

It's the kind that says, "I didn't choose all of it. But I do choose what I do with it."

Radical responsibility is the practice of holding your own power without shame, blame, or bypassing. It's not about blaming yourself for what you didn't know. It's about being brave enough to own what you do *now*.

It means taking stock of your life with unfiltered honesty:

That job you hate? *You stayed.*

That boundary that keeps getting crossed? *You haven't enforced it.*

That habit you swear, every Monday, you'll change? *Still there.*

Ouch. I know. Trust me, I *know*.

But here's the thing: this isn't about self-punishment. This is about *self-liberation*.

When you start taking radical responsibility, you stop being a character in someone else's script and start writing your own damn story.

It doesn't mean it's your fault. It means you've claimed your place as the one who can do something about it.

I remember the moment I finally *got* this, deep in my bones. I was sitting on the floor in my living room, surrounded by the chaos of a life that looked pristine from the outside and felt like a hostage situation on the inside.

And I thought, "No one's coming to save me." Actually, I screamed it to myself in my head, shaking myself awake into this honest reality.

No one is coming to save me. Only me.

Not because no one loves me. Not because I'm unworthy. But because this next season? It's mine to walk. Mine to lead. Mine to rebuild.

From that moment on, I started asking myself different questions:

What do I need to forgive myself for?

Where am I outsourcing my power?

What am I pretending not to know?

Radical responsibility is a reckoning. And a reclaiming.

It's the end of blame. It's the death of victimhood. It's the beginning of full, embodied, unapologetic choice.

And guess what? That's where your freedom lives.

This chapter isn't just about responsibility. It's about remembering this: *You are the one you've been waiting for.*

So go on. Pick up the pen. Start writing.

You're not broken. You're just in charge now.

∽

And here's where **INTEGRITY** steps in.

Integrity (noun):

Firm adherence to a code of especially moral or artistic values; incorruptibility; honesty. Also: The quality or state of being whole, entire, or undiminished.

Also: The quality or state of being whole, entire, or undiminished.

In simpler terms: Integrity is unity, an inner alignment between who you feel yourself to be and how you behave in the world. It's not about perfection. It's about being *undivided*, owning your values, speaking truth even when it's hard, and acting consistently when no one is watching.

Integrity isn't just a partner in responsibility; it's the vessel.

Without integrity, responsibility becomes hollow.

With it, responsibility becomes sacred.

Integrity means your internal world matches your external life. It's integrity behind closed doors, in the silent place where no one's watching, but the alignment matters most.

In Latin, *integer* means 'whole.' And real integrity lives in that wholeness, where your desires, decisions, and actions all speak the same truth.

It's not perfection; it's coherence. It's choosing the painful truth over easy comfort. It's showing up, again and again, even when convenience whispers otherwise.

Because integrity is radical responsibility made flesh.

It's more than owning your mistakes; it's keeping your agreements, speaking your truth, even when it's uncomfortable. Science ties integrity to higher emotional stability and life satisfaction; it anchors trust in yourself and with others. Without it, responsibility metabolises into guilt. With it, responsibility becomes power.

Ancient wisdom and modern thinkers echo it: *"With great power comes great responsibility,"* and with that responsibility must come integrity – or you fracture. When your internal ethic floods your external decisions, synchronicity shows up. Doors open. Trust forms. Alignment isn't just a feeling; it becomes magnetic.

Feeling your feelings matters here, too. Integrity requires that when your system is triggered, you don't bypass. You pause. You feel. You name. Then you respond. Not from shame or convenience, but from presence.

And there's courage in honesty, too. When you promise an email for Thursday, you send it – or you renegotiate. When you mess up, you admit it and make amends. You choose presence over pride. Small ruptures patched early save continents of regret later.

In your world, integrity is the glue that holds your pillars intact: wholeness, truth, depth, presence … they all crack when you don't live congruently. But when integrity holds, your life becomes an integrated field. That's the living manifesto.

Integrity is your invitation to be both powerfully aligned and endlessly human. It's owning your story, forging your sovereignty, and acting from coherence, not compromise.

So, carry this forward: Radical responsibility asked you to pick up the pen. Integrity teaches you to keep writing. To write from the whole, the true, the unwavering ground of *you*.

That's what comes next.

CHAPTER 9

THE GREAT RECLAMATION

Rebuilding the Self You Were
Always Meant to Be

Once the dust settles, the masks have been dropped, the truths are faced, and the ego has been kicked off its throne, you find yourself standing in a very strange place.

It's quiet here. Almost too quiet. Like the eerie calm after a storm, when you're not sure whether to exhale or brace yourself for the next wave. You've let go of so much of the old ... but haven't quite picked up the new yet.

This is the in-between.

The space between the unravelling and the rising. The sacred pause between death and rebirth. The moment after you've dropped the performance, but before you've reclaimed your power.

And it's confronting. Disorienting. It renders you vulnerable. *Because if you're no longer who you were ... who the hell are you?*

Welcome to The Great Reclamation.

This is not about reinvention. Reinvention is for brands. This is about *remembrance*.

It's where you stop striving to *become* something and start remembering who you were before the world told you who to be.

This is where the whispers get louder. Where the breadcrumbs become apparent. Where the version of you that's been buried beneath years of performing, pleasing, and proving finally begins to stir.

This is where you get to ask, "What parts of me were true before I became strategic?"; "What dreams did I silence so I wouldn't seem 'too much'?"; "What would my life look like if it were built around my soul, not my survival?"

It's where you gather the scattered, silenced, sensitive pieces of you and invite them to take up space again.

The real work of reclamation isn't glamorous. It's not all cacao ceremonies and curated journals. It's not about creating some perfectly aligned, aesthetically pleasing new identity.

It's about sitting in your shit and finally saying, "I'm not afraid to be here anymore."

It's about crying over the girl you abandoned to become palatable. It's about grieving the woman you *almost* became to make others comfortable. It's about looking at yourself in the mirror and seeing *her*. Not the mask, not the role, not the brand.

And then? It's about choosing her. Every damn day.

You begin to reclaim:

- Your voice, even when it trembles.
- Your truth, even when it doesn't fit the narrative.
- Your joy, without earning it.
- Your rest, without justifying it.

And slowly, what was once fragmented becomes whole again. Not perfect. But real.

You start laughing without checking the volume. You cry without apologising. You take up space at the table – and then you build your own.

You realise your power isn't in how much you can carry; it's in how deeply you can feel.

And that's when the magic starts to move.

Because when a woman reclaims herself, the world around her shifts. Not because she's forcing it. But because she *is* it.

The reclamation isn't loud. It's steady. It's sacred. It's slow. It's sovereign.

And if you're here now, half-raw, half-radiant, walking yourself home without a map … Welcome. You are not rebuilding. You are returning. And the person you're returning to?

She was never gone. *She was just waiting for you to remember.*

I understood something wild in that space where the Red and Blue began to bleed together. *Everything happens for a reason*. I understood it not as a neat slogan, but as an organic truth. Life wasn't happening *to* me; it was happening *for* me.

This realisation caused me an almost ridiculous level of discomfort at first – until it dawned on me that being uncomfortable was actually a good thing ... *because that was precisely where growth lived*. And so, I learned to be *comfortable* with being *uncomfortable*. I started leaning into the mess, the triggers, the unravelling, because that was where the truth seeped in.

I realised that the only way to maintain that feeling, that resonance of authenticity and presence, was to keep stretching, keep exploring deeper, keep healing every corner of what I'd buried. I was building my **DESTINED LIFE**, bit by painful, miraculous bit. I surrendered to the path that was unfolding, allowing the universe to guide me on the next step. I didn't force it. I leaned in.

In that surrender, one phrase landed so deeply it still hums in my bones: *amor fati* – love of one's fate – a Stoic concept revived by the German philosopher Friedrich Nietzsche, meaning to not just endure what life gives you, but to *embrace* it – joy, grief, chaos, wonder – as essential chapters in your 'becoming.'

The Stoic philosopher Marcus Aurelius wrote that "everything that happens, happens as it should"; Nietzsche challenged us to *love* that ideology. And that principle yielded a strategy for me to surrender. I stopped resisting the chaos and began welcoming it. I became a practitioner of deep work: body-based healing, emotional release, and ancestral deconditioning. I stepped into new roles. I became a Self-Directed Healing Practitioner, finding modalities that married spiritual clarity with actionable structure.

It wasn't clean. My beliefs shifted. My awareness deepened. I began noticing synchronicities everywhere, coincidences that felt too laden with meaning to ignore. For example, several of my friends or associates would mention a book I'd never heard of – and all of a sudden I inadvertently came across it; a particular number sequence would crop up repeatedly – on a number plate, the car radio clock, a billboard, then the time on my phone; a seemingly chance encounter felt destined, not random. I began to form the deep belief that: *There is something bigger than me at play here. I am part of a puzzle far greater than I can see.*

But paradox rose with potency. In the Red, I lived in empathy, in service, in feeling deeply. Yet in the Blue, I still built businesses, provided for my kids, controlled outcomes. In the Red, I felt clarity, purpose, calm … but I also suffered financial uncertainty, emotional overwhelm, and confusion. I traded structure for presence, but I found my boundaries dissolving too far. I became an adrenaline junkie of healing, pursuing trauma to fix it, chasing triggers for higher growth, until I realised that I couldn't maintain this state and run a life at the same time.

I was, in fact, living a *double life*. The Blue demanded my strategic mind; the Red demanded my open heart. I feared the Blue wouldn't accept the Red – and I needed the Blue to pay the bills. Meanwhile, I was craving love and belonging inside the Red, but felt more isolated than ever.

So, I asked myself, "Do I really have to choose one or the other? Must I choose a box?" It felt too reductive. Indoctrination had taught me to pick a lane. But I suddenly realised: *Wait a minute … I can be both. I MUST be both.* The push and pull – Blue and Red – is where the real learning pulses. That tension creates the *growth layer*.

And in that realisation, I made a choice. I decided not to box any part of me in, not to choose one side or another, but to hold both with integrity. I accepted that, yes, I lead with my heart, but I also carry structural responsibility. I could honour both parts of me – the corporate strategist and the spiritual empath. The earner and the healer.

That's the *paradox in polarity*. The becoming isn't about choosing one pole; it's about dancing between them with awareness, refusing to let one dominate. Living as *both* protects the higher truth – that none of us is linear. We are layered, messy, complex, and whole.

This is life with purpose. This is living *into* the paradox, not avoiding it. And through it all? *Amor fati* reminds me that not only is it okay, but it's essential, to love how this all unfolds. Every fade, every pivot, every tear. It builds the woman I came here to be.

CHAPTER 10

INTEGRATION

Becoming the Whole Damn You
(Without Needing to Prove It)

Integration. The part no one warns you about.

You've burned it all down. You've met your shadows. You've reclaimed your light.

Now what?

Now … you live it.

Which, let me be honest, is less like a Hollywood ending and more like a cosmic game of emotional Jenga.

Because integration isn't a ceremony. It's not a workshop. It's not something you can post about on Instagram with a crystal in your lap and a caption about 'alignment.'

Integration is Tuesday morning. Integration is school drop-off with puffy eyes and a regulated nervous system. Integration is choosing truth when denial would be easier. It's resting without guilt. It's setting boundaries without writing a whole thesis on why you're allowed to.

It's where the real flex is *consistency*, not intensity.

Where you stop explaining your growth and start embodying it.

And trust me, that's not always pretty. It's awkward. It's clunky. It's missing the meditation class because you needed a nap. It's forgetting everything you've learned mid-argument with your partner and coming back afterwards with, "Okay, let's try that again."

It's not perfection. It's integration.

It's the holy, human act of choosing again. And again. And again.

Because even when you know better, you will still fall. You'll still forget. You'll still have days where the ego tries to sneak back into the driver's seat with a triple-shot latte and a to-do list.

But here's the shift: Now you *notice*. Now you *name it*. Now you *choose differently*.

Integration means you don't shame yourself for the slip-ups; you honour yourself for the return.

You laugh at the mess. You celebrate the small wins. You know that one conscious breath is a miracle. That one honest "no" is revolutionary. That being gentle with yourself isn't weakness, it's wisdom.

Here's a moment I'll never forget …

It was a regular Wednesday. One of those mid-launch, mid-meltdown kind of weeks. The kids were bickering. Emails were exploding. I was already ten minutes late to a call with 'Someone Very Important who had Very Little Time.'

In my old life, I would've snapped. Rushed. Shoved everyone's feelings (and mine) to the side, squeezed into heels and hustle, and powered through with a fake smile and high-functioning burnout.

But that morning, something different happened.

I paused.

I crouched down, looked my daughter in the eye, and actually *heard* her. I wasn't thinking about the clock or the call or the KPI. I was *with* her.

And then, I did something unthinkable.

I rescheduled the meeting.

Not because someone was bleeding. Not because the house was on fire. But because *I mattered*. Because *presence* mattered. Because this moment in my hallway, with one of the little humans I love most, was more important than pretending to have it all together.

Old me would've called that weak. Integrated me knew it was power.

That was integration. Not at a retreat. Not on a stage. But in a hallway, with a choice.

When you do this, you no longer need to prove you've changed. *You are the evidence.*

This is where your life starts to feel like yours again. Not someone else's blueprint. Not a highlight reel. Not a brand strategy.

Just you. Living. Loving. Leading.

In your softness and your strength. In your knowing and your learning. In your wholeness.

This is integration. Not as a destination. But as a devotion.

And it's only the beginning.

∾

I began to notice the *space in between*, that soft tension hovering between my old self and who I was becoming. The part of me that wondered, *do I have to choose between becoming completely new or forever remaining the old version?* What if I just *was* ... me, holding the power and presence I had uncovered?

I had taken my power to radical levels in the Blue Pill realm: success, strategy, performance, full throttle. Now I found myself circling back, curious and open. Aware of my past but emboldened by possibility. I stepped into that liminal zone, between what was and what could be, holding both with intention. Because in that threshold lives creativity, growth, and transformation. (Liminality is literally the state of being betwixt and between.)

Many of us live uncomfortably in that middle space, torn between *false and true*, certainty and curiosity, right and wrong. What if your opinion differs from mine? Does that mean you're wrong, or I'm wrong? Does a different belief make you bad? Here's the truth: we are all one. We are separated only by ego, beliefs, and fear. When we pierce that illusion, unity reveals itself, stitched in synchronicity and shared humanity.

My beliefs shifted. I began to sense a higher Self, an internal guide that saw beyond identity and achievement. Those seemingly random signs and coincidences – synchronicities, such as receiving a message from someone just as I thought of that person, and that same number appearing in my life, again and again – took on more significance. My treasured concept of *amor fati* felt like an anchor. I was embracing the path exactly as it was unfolding, not as I *wished* it to be.

As I leaned into this new reality, I also forged a practical alignment. In my new role as a Self-Directed Healing Practitioner, I adopted a modality that stitched Red traits, such as compassion and presence, into a Blue brain that sought structure and impact. Suddenly *purpose*, *passion*, and *balance* were entire ecosystems, not abstract ideals.

And yes, the Red brought its shadows ... losing clarity, financial uncertainty, taking on others' pain. But in that middle space between Blue structure and Red intuition, I found the paradox: we don't need to be just one or the other. We can be both – a strategist and a healer; a business leader and an empath. That is the beauty of polarity. That's the refusal to be boxed in.

In that space between Blue and Red, I felt the pull of both worlds – career responsibilities and spiritual calling – and learned to hold them without collapsing into either. I still provided for my kids, ran my company, and held systems in place. At the same time, I nurtured stillness at home, presence with people, love without agenda. I stopped believing Blue wouldn't accept Red, or that I had to fully choose one over the other. I realised the real work, and liberation, lives in *integration*, not exclusion.

This is where integration arises. Not as compromise, but as evolution. It's what psychologists call *self-author-ship*: crafting a life guided by your inner voice rather than external formulas or inherited beliefs. It's stepping into the liminal: truth held without fear; ego recognised without override.

Do we really have to choose between new or old? Must we shrink parts of ourselves to fit someone else's story? Or can't we simply *grow into who we already are* by allowing both past and present to breathe in harmony?

That space in between isn't empty; it's fertile. Holding that tension with curiosity opens pathways we couldn't have seen from either pole alone. This is where integration lives, where head meets heart, strategy meets surrender, presence meets purpose. And that, my love … *that* is our Purple.

❧

So, what if I told you we can change our **BELIEFS**?

Hear me out.

Our beliefs create our behaviours. Those behaviours then craft our experiences, the very fabric of our lives.

We already know, deep down, that we're capable of shifting beliefs. We're not necessarily stuck with what we've been told or what we have absorbed. And if we can shape our beliefs, then we can recalibrate our behaviours.

Which means we can transform our experiences. Which means … we can shift our lives.

This isn't fluff. Psychology backs it up.

Our **core beliefs** act like mental templates, cognitive filters that decide how we see, respond, and show up (for better or worse) in our world. If you've ever found yourself behaving in ways that feel utterly out of alignment, yet familiar, because your brain is running on a belief track it inherited or absorbed long ago, you are not alone.

Here's the kicker: beliefs are not destiny. Social scientists confirm that our **self-efficacy**, our belief in our ability to act and change, is pivotal. Change those beliefs, and you automatically unlock new behavioural pathways and outcomes.

You can literally *shift the story you live*.

This is not just theoretical pie in the sky; it's the platform on which I rebuilt my life.

PART 3

THE PURPLE PILL - RADICAL TRANSFORMATION

CHAPTER 11

WHERE RED MEETS BLUE

Integration Meets Impact –
The Third Way Home

Here it is. The moment the whole journey has been leading to. The space where Red meets Blue. Where performance and presence sit at the same table. Where you no longer have to choose between success and self.

Because you get to hold both.

This is the Purple Pill. Not another pill to swallow, but a path to walk. Not a rejection of who you were, but a reintegration of all that you are.

The Purple Pill is the dance between doing and being. It's the permission to be strategic *and* soulful. Powerful *and* tender. Vision-led *and* heart-aligned.

It's what happens when you stop abandoning *yourself* for achievement and stop abandoning your dreams in the name of 'healing.'

It's a redefinition of success. Not by external metrics, but by internal alignment. Not by how loud the world claps, but by how deeply you know you are living true … true to yourself, that is.

Let me be clear here. The Purple Pill isn't balance. Balance is a myth designed to keep women doubting themselves.

This is *integration*.

This is *sovereignty*.

This is your life, not in compartments, but in colour.

The Purple Pill says,

- "I can be FIERCE in a boardroom and SOFT with my children."
- "I can LEAD with strategy and MOVE with intuition."
- "I can BUILD WEALTH … and still REST."
- "I can LAUNCH EMPIRES … and still take BUBBLE BATHS."

And none of it makes me less. In fact, it makes me *more*.

The Purple Pill is not perfection. It's wholeness. It's humanity. It's knowing when to hustle and when to halt. When to speak and when to listen. When to hold on and when to let go.

It's the woman who walks into a room with both edge and empathy, who doesn't shrink to be palatable or puff up to be powerful, who owns her story and leads from the scars, not in spite of them.

It's the leader you were always meant to be. The mother. The lover. The artist. The CEO. The healer. The truth-teller.

Not in conflict, but in collaboration.

This is the integration of all you've lived. This is the moment you stop choosing one path and start *creating your own.*

This is the Purple Pill.

∽

So, what does the Purple Pill look like?

It looks like saying "*no*" to a highpaying but soulnumbing project and saying "*yes*" to the one that lights you up, even if it doesn't fit your ego's logic.

It looks like walking into a meeting with your heart open and your mind sharp; being direct without being hard, clear without being cruel.

It looks like pausing before you react, breathing before you speak, and choosing to respond from the grounded, whole version of you, not the scared or scripted one.

It looks like building your business from your core values, not your wounds.

It looks like holding your child with presence – and leading a team with purpose.

It looks like being fully *you*, no matter the room.

I remember a time not long ago, standing on stage at a sold-out event. The old me would have rehearsed the talk

I was about to give twenty times, curated every slide, and calibrated every outfit for power signals – including shoulder pads.

But that day? I did the prep, sure ... but I let go of the performance.

I walked on stage with bare shoulders, steady breath, and nothing but the truth. My truth. I told *my* story. Not the polished version, but the real one. I didn't shrink. I didn't inflate. I simply *stood*.

Afterwards, a woman from the audience approached me with tears in her eyes. She said softly, "You just said what I've never had the words for."

That ... that right there? *That's Purple.*

The version of me that could command respect without needing to control everything. The version of me that could be powerful without performance. That chose *connection* over control.

That's what the Purple Pill unlocks.

It's not an aesthetic. It's a *frequency*. It's not a formula. It's a *felt sense*. It's not just healing. It's *embodiment*.

And the beauty of it all? It's already inside you.

It's the part of you that always knew you were meant for more. Not in a louder, shinier way, but in a deeper, truer way.

The Purple Pill doesn't give you something you never had. *It gives you back what you always had.*

It's the moment you finally realise, "I don't need to choose between who I love, what I do, and who I am. I get to bring *all* of me."

This is what choosing the Purple path means.
Welcome home.

∽

Why it matters

Research shows that people who align personal values with career goals experience higher satisfaction and purpose in their lives. Integrating spirituality and professional life increases not just emotional well-being, but commitment and clarity in decision-making.

This integrated inner alignment – Purple living – isn't just a metaphor; it's foundational in developmental psychology. *Psychosynthesis* encourages the uniting of the personal Self with the transpersonal Self, melding everyday living with spiritual depth.

The space between head and heart – the synergy of emotional intelligence and cognitive clarity – is where leaders thrive in the long term. And cultivating integration creates not only individual success but collective trust and well-being in teams and communities.

From psychology to spirituality, that space between the poles – between ambition and empathy, strategy and surrender, doing and being – is where real freedom, real creativity, real life *happens*.

That is the Purple Pill.

And it exists, in you, right now.

CHAPTER 12

COMING HOME

Wholeness Was Never Somewhere Else

Coming home. Not the white-picket-fence kind. Not the one with jazz music and fluffy slippers and candles burning in the background while you smile in slow motion.

I'm talking about the *real* kind of coming home. The kind where you're bruised but awake. Where the fire has stripped you bare and the silence echoes differently now. Where you look at yourself, *really* look, and see someone worth returning to. Not because she's perfect. But because she's *yours*.

This chapter isn't about the destination. It's about the return. The long walk back. The messy, sacred return to self.

The thing is, you don't realise how far you've drifted. Until the moment you land back inside your body and think, *Oh. There you are!*

For most of my life, I thought 'home' was something I had to earn. I thought I had to *become* something to deserve it. I thought I had to build the perfect business, be the perfect mother, keep the peace. Achieve, achieve, achieve … until maybe, one day, someone would tell me, "You made it."

But what I've learned, what this whole damn journey has shown me, is that there is no 'making it.' There is no finish line to becoming. There is only the remembering.

I remember the exact moment I felt *myself* drop back in. I was alone in the bath. No candles. No ambient playlist. No full moon ritual. Just me. My knees pulled up into my chest. Salt in the water. And tears streaming down my face. Not because I was broken, but because for the first time in forever … I *wasn't*.

I wasn't performing. I wasn't proving. I wasn't pushing.

I was simply *here*. In my skin. In my breath. In my truth.

And I realised something that changed everything: The woman I had been searching for, the one I had tried to curate, create, control … *she wasn't out there*. She was under it all. Under the masks. Under the hustle. Under the armour.

She had just been waiting … patiently … lovingly … for me to remember her.

Coming home doesn't look like a fairytale. It looks like ordinary moments that feel different because *you're* different.

It looks like laughing from your belly without wondering if it's too loud. It looks like saying "I don't know" and not needing to apologise for it. It looks like choosing rest without guilt, desire without shame, truth without explanation.

It looks like walking past a mirror and smiling, not at the perfection, but at the *presence*.

It's reclaiming the moments you once missed because you were too busy being impressive.

It's learning how to be with yourself in the quiet and not feel the need to fill it.

It's waking up and realising, "I am safe now. I am soft now. I am strong now."

Not because someone handed it to you. But because you *earned* it. Not through proving, but through returning.

You burned the blueprint. You questioned the code. You picked up every shattered piece and asked, "What stays, what goes, and what was never mine to carry?"

And now? Now you stand in a life that might not be as tidy, but which is *true*.

You don't owe anyone the performance anymore. You don't need the applause. You don't need to be saved.

You are no longer the version of you who settled for *almost*. Who shrank for comfort. Who contorted for approval.

You are the woman who came back.

Fully. Finally. Unapologetically.

So, if you're standing here now, blinking in the softness, stretching into the spaciousness …

Welcome home, love. You made it. Not to 'the end.' But to the truth.

And that is everything.

❦

Let's get one thing straight, though. Coming home to yourself isn't a one-time arrival. It's a sacred cycle. A continuous practice. A lifelong devotion. And if you're wondering how to stay there, how to root in, return to, and remain connected to your inner home, here are a few guiding lights that have helped me over and over again.

It begins with **awareness**. Not a vague "I think something feels off," but a fierce, clear-eyed willingness to *see*. To see the patterns that keep playing out. The relationships that feel like déjà vu. The situations that keep you spinning.

Start with just one. One key area of your life that keeps pulling you out of alignment. Maybe it's your relationship. Your work. Your health. Your sense of worth.

Zoom in.

Then ask,

- **"Why** am I here?"
- **"What** am I believing about myself in this situation?"
- **"Who** do I become when I'm in this loop?"
- **"How** am I contributing to it, consciously or not?"

This is the power of **observation**. When we stop reacting and start witnessing, we step outside the chaos and into clarity. Observation doesn't mean judgement. It means curiosity. It means taking the bird's-eye view, rising above the noise, and seeing the full picture.

When we see it all clearly – our part, their part, the deeper pattern – we unlock something powerful: **forgiveness**. Forgiveness for them, maybe. But more importantly, for ourselves. For the versions of us that didn't know better. For the times we abandoned ourselves for approval, for safety, for survival.

When we see clearly, we can *choose* clearly. And that's when we grow.

Growth isn't just about adding new habits or breaking old ones. It's about healing what we've ignored. About telling the truth in places we've stayed silent. About finally saying "no more" when our spirit has been whispering it for years.

Growth hurts, sometimes. It's uncomfortable. But it's always worth it. Because on the other side of growth comes something we've all been craving:

Clarity. That moment when the fog lifts. When you suddenly know why it all had to happen the way it did. When you realise the chaos wasn't punishment, it was a portal. When you feel the click inside your chest that says, *"This is the path forward. This is who I'm becoming."*

And once that clarity lands? Something else opens:

Gratitude. Gratitude not just for the wins, but for the wounds. For the heartbreaks, the failures, the mess. Because without them, you wouldn't have cracked open.

You wouldn't have looked deeper. You wouldn't have found your way *home*.

You look back and think, "Damn. I did that. I lived through that. I became someone I'm actually proud of."

Because let's be honest … healing isn't a checklist. Growth isn't a Pinterest board. Real, *lasting* change doesn't come from reading the right book or booking the next retreat.

It comes from becoming the kind of person who lives in alignment when no one is watching. The kind of person who *embodies* change, not just talks about it. The kind of person who leads their life, not by the wound, but by the wisdom.

This is not about perfection. This is about *participation*.

In your own life. In your own becoming. In your own return. It starts inside of you. It starts now.

YOU are the magic. YOU are the one with the wand. YOU get to decide what this next season of life looks like.

Not for your parents.

Not for your partner.

Not for strangers on the internet.

For *you*.

You get to show your children what self-trust looks like. You get to love your people without abandoning your own needs. You get to rise, fall, rise again, and still be worthy every step of the way.

We only get one shot at this life. So, take it. With both hands. With your full heart.

And if you're ever unsure where to start?

Start here.

Start now.

Start with just a little bit more Purple.

CHAPTER 13

THE INTEGRATION PILLARS

Living It, Every Damn Day

Once you've come home to yourself, walked through the Blue, stood under the Red, and found the Purple, the real question emerges:

How do you *stay* here?

Because transformation isn't a trophy to be claimed; it's a practice, a devotion. And the only way to remain aligned, awake, and whole is to *return*, again and again and again.

That's why I introduced the **Integration Pillars**: not rules, not mandates, but *anchors* ... steady, unwavering, affirming.

What are Pillars? In the Merriam-Webster definition, a *pillar* is *"a firm upright support ... a supporting, integral, or upstanding member or part."* Think of ancient temples. Their grand ceilings never collapse. Why? Because the pillars that support them stand strong.

And that's what these are. Not fences. Not tick-boxes. Not yet more self-help gimmicks. They don't *fix* you. They *hold* you. They remind you who you are when everything else tries to shift. So here they are, my eight pillars of integration:

The 8 Pillars of Integration

1. Wholeness over Perfection

You're not a project to complete; you're a soul to *live*. When you stumble, come back gently.

2. Truth over Image

Authenticity builds bridges; polish builds walls. Show your edges; they hold light.

3. Depth over Décor

Ask the questions. Have the uncomfortable conversations. Risk clarity over comfort.

4. Alignment over Approval

You don't need validation, you need direction. Let your internal compass guide you.

5. Rest is Power

Rest isn't earned; it's essential. You're worthy of it, irrespective of your output.

6. Presence is Everything

You're not here to tick boxes, you're here to *be* here. Your breath, your body, your life, fully.

7. Self before Service

You can't pour from an empty cup. Nurture yourself first. Not because it's selfish, but because it's sacred.

8. You Already Know!

Your body remembers. Your intuition whispers. *Your truth doesn't need convincing.*

∾

A True Moment of Pillar Living

Let me tell you about choosing **Depth over Décor** at a community event. Picture me: stage-ready, laser-focused on optics, hiding the hollowness inside. I was supposed to be networking, but something inside me nudged: *Ask a question that opens a heart.*

I leaned into the person I was talking to and said, "How are *you*, really?"

Crickets. Then tears. Then, the beautiful soul beside me broke down and whispered, "I've been drowning." Not metaphorically, but, quite literally, burnout. Desperate texts at 3 am; exhaustion that never showed on the outside.

We held space in that hallway, without pretending. There was no branding. No agenda. Just real presence.

That moment wasn't content marketing; it was *medicine*. I didn't gain followers; I gained kinship. Integration lives in those unfiltered, tender borders.

Your Turn: Reflection Prompts

Fold these into your day:

1. Which pillar calls to you today?
2. How can you lean into it, just once, in some small way?
3. What's your next micro-step? An intention, a boundary, a breath?

❧

Why These Pillars Matter

They matter because you will forget. You will slip into habits of old. You will shrink into performance. That's human.

But with these pillars? They *remember* who you are. They're not just spiritual slogans; they're muscle memory. They're a whispered **"I've got me"** when the world pushes. They're soft returns when the ground shakes.

Integration isn't final; it's *fierce*. It's not one grand leap, but a thousand homecomings. Each press into one pillar is a step towards the woman you came back for. Not better; *braver*.

You don't need to *fix* your life. You need to *fill* it … with courage, clarity, and choice. And each time you live the pillars, you're not just staying; you're *soaring*.

Welcome home.

CHAPTER 14

THE NEW STANDARD

Your Manifesto for a Life Unleashed

Now, at the end of this journey, you stand not at a finish line, but at a beginning. What you need is a declaration. A manifesto. A sacred statement of who you are, what you believe, and the world you're calling in.

What is a manifesto?

According to Merriam-Webster, a manifesto is *"a written statement declaring publicly the intentions, motives, or views of its issuer."* It's not a marketing tagline; it's a soul declaration. A call to arms of the heart. A verbal monument to your becoming.

This is your **New Standard**: an embodied manifesto, not just to read, but to *become*.

The Standard I Stand For

1. Whole-hearted Living

I will no longer choose compliance over courage, convenience over clarity. I will say "yes" to presence and "no" to anything that dims my truth.

2. Radical Integrity

I will speak my truth, even when my voice shakes. I do not need to be liked. I will be *felt*.

3. Brave Softness

I will lead with both strength *and* tenderness. I will show up with boundaries and hold space for others to be human.

4. Purpose-Fuelled Action

I will build and create from soul, not from scarcity. Every vision I chase will carry heart as its engine.

5. Joyful Abundance

I believe abundance is fertile ground, not measured by possessions, but by presence. I claim rest, play, and pleasure as rights, not rewards.

6. Courage to Return

When I stumble or sink, I choose to get up. I don't reset. I *remember*. I return to my pillars. My path is cyclical, not linear.

7. Generosity over Gain

I will uplift with my legacy. My success doesn't come at someone else's cost. I leave room. I empower. I make space at the table.

8. Community as Core

I will move with my people, not in spite of them. I will show up for collective dreaming, collective healing, and collective truth.

Why This Matters

Declaring this isn't vanity. It's sovereignty.

When you stand behind your standards – live them, breathe them, speak them into existence – you attract the life you respect. You stop chasing applause. You start living for impact. For freedom. For peace.

A manifesto isn't just a document; it's a direction.

A compass when life gets loud.

A foundation when everything else feels shaky.

Your Invitation

Now it's your turn.

Take a page, a pen, and your truth, and declare:

- Who you are becoming.
- What you will *no longer tolerate*.
- What you *now demand* in your life.

Write it fiercely and clearly: *"I stand for..."*
"I embody..."

"I refuse..."

"I choose..."

Hold it close. Circulate it. Infuse it into your days. Let it guide your speech, your decisions, your relationships.

This Isn't Over. It's Just Begun

Your journey has not ended with integration. It begins with your **irrevocable right to choice**.

> This manifesto isn't a file to archive.
>
> It's the fuel for your free life.
>
> It's the platform for your power.
>
> It's the declaration of your destiny.
>
> Move forward inhabited.
>
> Move forward aligned.
>
> Move forward unwavering.

Because this is your **New Standard**, a way of life built from wholeness, carried by your soul, and anchored in legacy. It's the final chapter you *live*, not just read.

Welcome to the world you've been preparing to create.

Welcome to the life that waits for no one but you.

You are the manifesto.

A LOVE LETTER

Dear Beloved Self,

Remember when you stood at the beginning of this book bright-eyed but burdened, powerful yet paused, wearing armour to feel safe and silence to feel seen? I remember. I remember you in boardrooms that felt like cages, in moments of triumph that rang hollow, and in that still, small voice whispering, *"There has to be more."*

I am writing to you now from a place of deeper certainty and softer strength. I am you at the end of this journey, a version of you who has dared to remember, to feel, to return. I've walked through the Blue, stumbled into the Red, found the Purple, and now I stand grounded in my truth.

I want you to know this: you did not fail on the way here. You were brave enough to begin. You were curious enough to continue. You were wise enough to say *enough* – and choose you.

Here are a few things I wish you knew:

You are always enough, even on the days the phone doesn't ring, the inbox is empty, or the applause is silent. Your worth isn't tied to output; it's woven into your DNA.

Vulnerability is your power. Every tear, every tremble, every moment you showed up in your mess, it became the soil for deeper belonging.

Holding two seemingly opposite truths doesn't break you; it completes you. You can be loud and tender, strategic and intuitive, grounded and expansive, and this tension is your liberation.

Your impact isn't measured by your reach. It's measured by your *realness*. The lives you've touched in the hallway, the hearts you've held in the hard.

This life is sacred, this *ordinary* life. Family dinners, breathy laughter, slow mornings. These moments are not detours; they are your path.

You get to choose, again and again. Even if you stray, or stall, or stand still, you get to return. That is your freedom.

Trust yourself. Your body, your boundaries, your wholeness. They are your compass. If it feels off, it *is* off. If you thirst for something deeper, you *are* thirsty … for alignment, for freedom, for depth.

You've already done the hardest part. You looked at the broken ceilings and said, *"Not on my watch."* You leapt into the unknown. You *leaned* into your edges. You chose not just to survive, but to *thrive* as your own saviour.

As I write, I see you there, bracing for greatness while hiding your softer parts. I see you building legacies while forgetting to live. I see you dancing on edges, all the while afraid to step into stillness.

So, here's what I want for you now:

- Lean into the quiet as deeply as you lean into the roar.
- Give yourself room to rest without apology.
- Speak the truth you feel, not just the story you think people want.
- Let your guard down, even when it's scary; it's where trust lives.
- Choose love over performing. For yourself, your life, your legacy.

There is no more chasing. Not of perfection, not of proof, not of praise. There is only *becoming*. Fully. Fiercely. Humanly.

Thank you for taking the first step – back to yourself, and forward, into wholeness. I stand with you, beside you, within you, with all the grace and grit that got us here.

Welcome home, beloved. We are ready.

With all my love,

You xx

BEYOND THE PAGES - LIFE IN THE PURPLE

This story has now reached its summit. The journey's arc – Blue, Red, Purple, and coming home – has been completed. But as any wise storyteller knows, the epilogue isn't a final bow; it's a soft exhale, a breath held and released, a gentle invitation to *live* what you, dear reader, have spoken into the world.

A Few Years Later

I'm sitting in my sunlit backyard, legs tucked under me, half-drinking a coffee that's gone cold because I got distracted. Again. My daughter hums beside me as she paints rocks for the garden.

The world outside is still busy.

But here, in our little oasis, it's peaceful. Real. Unfiltered.

The calendar still fills. The inbox still pings. But there's room now. There's pause. *There's me.*

The Purple in Action

I turn down a speaking gig that pays well but doesn't feel aligned, with no guilt.

I start every workday with ten breaths, grounding myself into purpose before productivity.

On Wednesdays, I close my laptop by 5 pm. I call it Soul Night, a quiet ritual of no agenda – just presence.

I sit with my partner deeply, not just politely, sometimes arguing, sometimes igniting, always connected.

And yes, sometimes I choose popcorn and PJs over high-performance planning, even in this so-called 'launch' phase.

That's the integration I live now. Not learned, but embodied. Not theoretical, but tangible. Not temporary, but sustained. Real life in full colour.

What *Your* Epilogue Is For

An epilogue isn't a rewrite of the ending. It's not another opportunity to prove. It's the space where you breathe into what you did and what continues to unfold.

It's a soft, lived update on who you've become and how you'll continue. An answer to readers wondering, "What becomes of her now?" It's not Hemingway's perfection. It's not Rowling's *19 Years Later*. It's your everyday life, among the real Real.

It shows that transformation isn't a flash; it's a foundation. That change doesn't end; it evolves. That the story you've read is not boxed or bound; it breathes outside the lines.

Looking Forward

Will there still be hard mornings? Yes. Will self-sabotage knock? Of course. Will perfectionism peek back in? That's part of the deal.

But the difference? When the old patterns whisper, "Return to Blue," there are the Pillars. There's a manifesto. There's a voice at home saying, "No, love. Not today."

Final Whisper

Your transformation wasn't a 'nice-to-have'; it was a calling. This epilogue isn't an ending; it's a beginning. It's the quiet exhale after the climb. It's the first sunrise of your own unfolding.

So, breathe. Stay soft. Hold your truth.

And, if you'll allow, continue to live it.

Because the best part of the story isn't behind us; it's happening now.

Welcome to life after the story.

Lots of love,

Kiani xxx

ABOUT THE AUTHOR

Kiani Mills is a multi-faceted entrepreneur, mentor, and author whose life's work is dedicated to helping people transform the way they live, lead, and do business. She is the founder of Imperiale Conveyancing, one of the first Australia-wide conveyancing-only firms, and the creator of *The Purple Pill* philosophy – a groundbreaking approach that fuses strategy (the Blue Pill) with mindset and mastery (the Red Pill) to create true alignment and transformation (the Purple Pill).

Kiani's journey has been anything but linear. From single motherhood to scaling multiple businesses, from deep personal losses to spiritual awakenings, she has walked through the fire and chosen to turn her scars into service. Her voice is raw, unfiltered, and unapologetically real, inviting readers, clients, and audiences to meet themselves with honesty, courage, and heart.

Beyond business, Kiani is the founder of several initiatives that honour her late sister, Courtney Mills, including PROJECT 100, women-in-music grants, and industry collectives designed to break down barriers and build communities of support. Her work extends across industries and countries but is always anchored in one mission: to empower people to design life and business by choice, not by default.

Kiani lives on the Sunshine Coast in Australia with her two children, who remain her greatest teachers and her deepest 'Why.'